Exposing the Queen of Heaven

eXposing the Queen of Heaven

Vinny Gallagher

Belleville, Ontario, Canada

Exposing the Queen of Heaven

Copyright © 2001, Vinny Gallagher
Cover Design by Carl Weiss

All Scripture quotations, unless otherwise specified, are taken from the *New International Version* of the Bible (Copyright 1973, 1978, 1984 International Bible Society. Used by permission of Zondervan Bible Publishers.

Scripture quotations marked KJV, are from *The Holy Bible, King James Version*. Copyright © 1977, 1984, Thomas Nelson Inc., Publishers.

Scripture quotations marked NKJV are taken from the *New King James Version*. Copyright © 1979, 1980, 1982. Thomas Nelson Inc., Publishers.

ISBN: 1-55306-306-6

First printing, December 2001
Second printing, March 2003

FOR MORE INFORMATION CONTACT:

Vinny Gallagher
Box 123
Honey Brook, Pennsylvania
19344-0123
(610) 415-0115
e-mail: Jesuslovesu4ever@juno.com

Guardian Books is an imprint of *Essence Publishing,* a Christian Book Publisher dedicated to furthering the work of Christ through the written word.
For more information, contact:
20 Hanna Court, Belleville, Ontario, Canada K8P 5J2.
Phone: 1-800-238-6376 • Fax: (613) 962-3055
E-mail: publishing@essencegroup.com
Internet: www.essencegroup.com

Printed in Canada
by

Chapter One

ANCIENT DECEPTION

The scene has replayed itself through the years: an apparition of a beautiful woman appears, usually over a grove of trees or near a spring of water. The apparition declares herself to be God's mother, or God's spouse, or the Mother of the gods, and demands veneration, obedience, and worship. Promises are made by the apparition, secrets are given to the young seers, and miracles often occur.

The beautiful woman demands that a temple be erected to her. She warns of a coming judgment. Obedience to her wishes will bring salvation to all who will heed her words, she declares.

The ancient world was filled with devotion to this apparition. Her statues littered the ancient landscape, and her shrines and temples were everywhere. Even the people of God, the Israelites, turned from the true worship of God to this apparition.

Have you ever wondered who were the demon idols that caused Israel to turn from the Lord God? One of the foremost demons was this very apparition: the Queen of Heaven.

Even King Solomon, builder of the temple in Jerusalem, turned to several idols, and especially venerated the Queen of Heaven alongside of the one true God of Israel:

...Solomon king of Israel had built for Ashtoreth the vile goddess [an altar] **(2 Kings 23:13).**

Elijah, the prophet, spoke to the wicked King Ahab:

"You have abandoned the LORD's commands and have followed the Baals. Now summon the people from all over Israel to meet me on Mount Carmel. And bring the four hundred and fifty prophets of Baal and the four hundred prophets of Asherah, who eat at Jezebel's table" (1 Kings 18:18).

The divine Mother, known variously as the "Queen of Heaven" or "Asherah," was one of the ancient world's main idols, and the demon behind it still reigns in many parts of the world. Her influence in modern-day Christianity is significant and would shock many believers.

Some people have been taught that the biblical Mary has been supernaturally appearing with a message from God. The apparition appears and tells people that she was born without original sin. She says that she is a co-mediator and co-redeemer of humanity. She tells people to pray to her, to dedicate themselves and their loved ones to her, and to perform religious works of obedience to her. She proclaims herself to be the Queen of Heaven and the Mother of God.

But is the woman who has been supernaturally appearing actually the historic Mary of Scripture? Is the teaching that the apparition brings in accordance with Scripture? Or is the spirit behind the apparitions a demonic imposter? And if so, what are the consequences for those who have invited this spirit into their hearts? Is the demon, formerly known as "Asherah" to the ancients, now masquerading as "Mary"?

Visitations of a woman who declares herself to be the "Queen of Heaven" have appeared throughout history, even before the Christian era. She usually appears to children, asks them to dedicate themselves to her, requires that they build her an altar or temple, and presents teachings about herself for them to spread throughout the earth. Whole countries have been formally consecrated to this ghost-like personality. Her cult of followers are very loyal and zealous for what the other-worldly figure tells them to do.

In the Christian era, this same spirit continues to appear, yet she has given herself a new name that she would like to be known as: Mary, from the Bible.

In this booklet, we will identify the true identity of the apparitions of "Mary." We will show how she has been appearing since before the Christian era and will reveal through Scripture how idolatry, even that which was performed in ignorance, fear, or superstition, can release penalties that can affect us, even after we become born-again Christians.

Best of all, we will offer practical help on how to break any curse that may be on your finances, relationships, or health, as a result of any consecrations made to the Queen of Heaven over you.

Chapter Two

BABYLON REVISITED

The ancient demonic deities that deceived Israel have not gone away, but they have just changed their names. Christian historian and researcher George Otis, Jr. calls this an "adaptive deception."[1] In other words, they are the same demons, but they are operating under different names. These demons don't care what people call them, as long as they can take devotion away from God Himself.

As a form of state-sponsored Christianity swept through regions by forced conversions in the 4th and 5th century, A.D., the apparitions of this ancient "Mother" spirit continued—same woman, same message, same "secrets" and occult miracles. Only now, she gave herself a new name to deceive the newly converted Christians. She told them that she was Mary, the Mother of God. People venerated her, shrines were built, and temples erected. Her statue was placed in Christian churches for adoration, inspiration, and veneration. Her worship continued down the same family lines in which she had been worshiped for generations—same demon, different name, but holding the same illegal influence in their souls.

The ancient Mother goddess had told the people that she was "immaculately conceived." Both the ancient Greek goddess Hera and the Roman goddess Juno appeared to the ancients and told them to celebrate the "Feast of the Immaculate Conception" every March 25th. Interestingly, it was on March 25th that this same demonic apparition appeared at Lourdes, France, and declared to the world once again, "I am the Immaculate Conception."

Throughout the Christian era, the apparition sought to dictate theology in the Christian Church. She brought forth new doctrines that had no basis in Scripture, but which were founded on her words alone and the miracles she performed.

Who is this spirit? Are her words in accordance with the Word of God? Or does she present another gospel?

We will identify the various names that this apparition has assumed throughout the centuries, and we will then look at the messages she brings and compare them to Scripture.

After we expose this apparition and judge her messages in the light of Scripture, we will lead you into a renunciation of her, which will free you of any of the lasting effects she may have upon your soul.

> **"So do not pray for this people nor offer any plea or petition for them; do not plead with me, for I will not listen to you. Do you not see what they are doing in the towns of Judah and in the streets**

of Jerusalem? The children gather wood, fathers light the fire, and the women knead the dough and make cakes of bread for the Queen of Heaven. They pour out drink offerings to other gods to provoke me to anger. But am I the one they are provoking? declares the LORD. Are they not rather harming themselves, to their own shame?" (Jeremiah 7:16-19).

The false Mary that is appearing today is none other than the same Queen of Heaven that is exposed in the Bible. The Queen of Heaven was a seductive and manipulative demon in Scripture, who appeared to the people and deceived them by miraculous signs. She is also known as "Asherah." She desires a throne and wants to exert her control over people.

Ishtar of Babylon is the Queen of Heaven mentioned by Jeremiah. She was married to Ba'al, the sun god. She was known throughout the ancient world as the moon goddess. That is why even now, masquerading as Mary, she often appears atop a crescent moon. This demon is also behind Islam who uses the crescent moon as its symbol.

The Israelites called her "Ashtoreth." She was also known as "Astarte" in the Mid-East. Her cult objects were known as "Asherah poles," and her ancient statues resemble modern-day statues of Mary.

She was known and worshiped throughout the ages in every civilization and was known variously as:

1. "Astarte" to the Canaanites
2. "Ashtoreth" to the Hebrews
3. "Isis" to the Egyptians

4. "Diana" of Ephesus
5. "Aphrodite" to the Greeks
6. "Juno" and "Venus" to the Romans

She appeared to the pagan Europeans, and was known as "Easter." Her message throughout the ages is the same: "I am your Mother; I have influence over God; you must obey me, build me an altar, open your hearts to me, etc.

She had a very loyal following amongst the people, for she stirred in them their natural love for the mother figure. She also took advantage of their ignorance and sentimentality to get them to consecrate themselves to her. They, in turn, quickly began to venerate her, pray to her, and consecrate themselves to her protection. She performed many dramatic signs and wonders for them, including physical healings.

This mother spirit was very persuasive and seductive. She would often appear weeping, telling the people that their bad deeds had made her sad, but if they built her a temple she would be pleased. As well, she often appeared with a baby in her arms, who was supposedly her divine son, or she told them that her divine spouse was angry and that they should offer their lives to her care. It was obvious that she was seeking a throne, but it was also obvious that the people were eager to fulfill her wishes. In Egypt, Isis was referred to as the "Sorrowful Mother," or "She who weeps," as she often appeared crying for the sins of the people. Eventually in Rome, this same spirit would reveal herself as "Mary," or "Mater Dolorosa," Latin for "Sorrowful Mother."

Even Christians can take on some of the attributes of the "Sorrowful Mother." It is important to get free of soulish sorrow in our own lives. The "Sorrowful Mother" demon is closely linked with the spirit of control, seduction, worldly sorrow, manipulation, the Anti-Christ, Death, deception, soulish enthusiasm, and the spirit of Jezebel. She is also connected to the "Eye of Horus," the "All-Seeing Eye" of occult religion.

Whatever her given name—Isis, Ishtar, Asherah—it is all the same demonic spirit that is still appearing to people throughout the Church age and is now calling herself "Mary, the Mother of God." She is a very strong international demonic principality.

Within the cult of Ishtar, one can see the amazing parallel to the modern day cult of Mary. Once you have come to recognize her and all that accompanies her veneration, her present day disguises will become transparent.

The following table, compiled by Patti Ponikvar in her unpublished manuscript, *Beyond Babylon*, best displays the striking resemblances.

ISHTAR	"MARY"
• Queen of Heaven • Mother of Men • Queen of Heaven and Earth • Refuge of Sinners • Morning Star	• Queen of Heaven • Mother of Men • Queen of Heaven and Earth • Refuge of Sinners • Morning Star
ISIS	"MARY'
• Mother of God • Our Lady • Star of the Sea • Lady of Wisdom	• Mother of God • Our Lady • Star of the Sea • Mother of Wisdom

ISIS	"MARY'
• Spouse of God • Queen Enthroned • Virgin Mother Immaculately Conceived • She Who Weeps	• Bride of the Father • Queen Enthroned • Virgin Mother Immaculately Conceived • The Sorrowful Mother
Other Similarities	**Other Similarities**
• She was patroness of cities and countries • She was goddess of springs of water • Depicted with crescent moon under foot • Appeared with a small child in arms • Weeping statues miraculously shed tears • Ishtar said she was a refuge for sinners • Ishtar bestowed life, health, and blessing • Without Ishtar, none could possess peace • Eight-pointed star was one of her emblems • Temples were built to her in cities • Wore a veil, crown, and sash	• She is patroness of cities and countries • She almost always appears by a spring • Depicted with crescent moon under foot • Madonna, the Mother and Son • Weeping statues miraculously sheds tears • This is taught of Mary as well • Mary is the source of all blessings • Mary is the "Queen of Peace" • Eight-pointed star on icons of Mary • Mary still asks for temples and shrines • Identical description of apparition's garb

These similarities are not coincidences. They are part of the trail of clues that this spirit has left behind as it has tried to deceive the nations.

This demonic spirit always required the people to make a statue, design beads, or wear a badge of some sort to connect them to her. They were taught that if they trusted in these objects and her power behind them, they would be saved. Those familiar with the world of the occult know them as "amulets" and "fetishes."

The statues of herself, the rosary, the miraculous medal, the scapular, and other occult items that this demon has commanded her followers to make and wear, are all defiling objects. They are "points of contact" or "gates," which connect someone intimately to the influence of this beguiling spirit.

These items must be destroyed, for they are accursed objects and will attract demonic spirits.

> "And you, by all means abstain from the accursed things, lest you become accursed when you take of the accursed things…" (Joshua 6:18 NKJV).

ASHERAH UNVEILED

Ishtar, or Astarte (Asherah), as the Israelites called her, appeared over springs of water or in or above groves of trees, just as she still does today. In Lourdes, she appeared and made a spring of water come forth from the ground. Asherah is translated "groves" in 2 Kings 21:17 and 2 Chronicles 15:16.

The Asherah pole, or tree, was believed to be a doorway

to her. This is where the old superstition of "knock on wood," a phrase for good luck, originates.

To "knock on wood" was to inquire of Ashtoreth, to beseech her with petitions, prayers, requests, and offerings. The making of hot cross buns at Easter (Ishtar) is a throwback to the offerings made to this goddess. Shrines and altars to Asherah were always placed near trees, or in groves of trees, and Marian shrines are still placed there today, now called "Grottoes."

Asherah was the consort (wife/lover) of Baal and was the deity that Elijah confronted on Mt. Carmel in Israel. It is interesting that an altar was built to Mary on the top of this same mountain in the 12th century, A.D. An order of Carmelites was established, and the Asherah (Mary) appeared to Simon Stock, one of the members of this order and gave him an occult object—the scapular. In one appearance, she goes so far as to declare that the amulets (points of contact with her spirit) can bring salvation to the wearer!

"Here is the privilege I grant to you and all the children. ... Whoever dies clothed in this scapular shall be saved." [2]

The deceived followers of the false "Mary" (Asherah) are led to think that superstitiously believing in a cloth will save them. The true Word of God declares that we cannot be saved by wearing supernaturally-crafted clothing. Only a personal faith in Jesus Christ and what His death at Calvary accomplished can save us. For the Scriptures clearly state that,

...it is by grace you have been saved, through faith—and this not from yourselves, it is the gift

of God—not by works, so that no one can boast (Ephesians 2:8-9).

Of course, the Asherah never preaches the true gospel of Jesus, but only a perverted mixture of works and idolatry mingled with Christian themes.

Sadly, on Mt. Carmel today stands a statue of the Queen of Heaven nestled in a grove of trees, as she always was. It seems as if the ancient enemy of Elijah is still around!

What has been will be again, what has been done will be done again; there is nothing new under the sun. Is there anything of which one can say, "Look! This is something new"? It was here already, long ago; it was here before our time (Ecclesiastes 1:9-10).

In another famous apparition at Guadelupe, Mexico, she (Our Lady of Guadelupe) proclaims,

…build me a Temple…am I not your Mother? You do not need anything else![3]

The Lord has made it clear regarding His prohibition concerning this type of worship. He says,

1.) You shall have no other gods before Me (Deuteronomy 5:7).
2.) You shall not make an image to bow down and worship (Deuteronomy 5:8-9).
3.) You shall not worship the Lord your God with such things (Deuteronomy 12:4).
4.) You shall not worship Me in this way (Deuteronomy 12:31).

Many "good" or "religious" people have a hard time accepting that their religion may be idolatrous, but the results of idolatry are always clear, even when it is committed in ignorance, or even with good intentions. Whenever someone in our family, even back to the previous third or fourth generation, commits idolatry and does not repent, the Bible says a curse may be laid on the family line.

Some examples of Marian idolatry include, but are not limited to:

- Saying prayers to Mary and trusting her instead of, or in addition to, Father, Son, or Holy Spirit
- Keeping a statue (idol) of her in the home, honoring it, or placing flowers by it
- Bowing the knee in obeisance to her at a wedding ceremony or prayer event
- Placing flowers at her altar, bowing at an altar to her, praying before her altar
- Wearing the scapular and trusting in its "power" to save you
- Trusting in the power of the "Miraculous Medal."
- Consecrating oneself or others to her through prayer

The curses released because of unrepentant idolatry in our family line may include:

- Marital and family problems; family estrangements.
- Chronic financial problems
- Mental illness, depression, anxiety attacks, etc.
- Premature death
- Chronic sickness
- Female problems
- Being accident prone
- Ongoing victimization of various sorts

(See list of blessings and curses in Deuteronomy 28:15-68.)

CURSED FOR IDOLATRY?

Although the original list of curses were spelled out for Israel, spiritual principles and dynamics can apply even today. Although God does not bring correction and repentance to His people to condemn them, He desires for us to be instructed in His truth and to become more like Him.

In Christ, these curses can be broken, because Christ became a curse that we might receive a blessing. We have now the grace to turn from all idolatry through repentance and faith in Him alone. Although the actions of our past, or those of our parents, may not keep us from salvation, they can affect the quality of our lives here on earth.

Even believers can be prone to generational curses. The good news is that we can break curses by faith in Christ and can dismiss these demons. No demon can abide in your spirit where His Holy Spirit dwells. But they can afflict, harass, tempt, torment, persecute, oppress, and attempt to destroy aspects of your soul or body. In order to understand deliverance for believers, one must understand the difference between the soul, the spirit, and the body. Although the believer's spirit is one with the Lord and is off-limits to the demonic, their soul (mind, will, and emotions) can be affected by demons, as well as their body:

> **May God himself, the God of peace, sanctify you through and through. May your whole spirit, soul and body be kept blameless at the coming of our Lord Jesus Christ. The one who calls you is faithful and he will do it (1 Thessalonians 5:23).**

Some say that a believer doesn't have to deal with the

demonic within themselves. But we know that although Christ purchased deliverance for us on Calvary, we must accept it by faith, resist the devil, and allow God to conform us into the image of His Son. Whatever within us is not like Christ must go! The Word is clear that the devil, the flesh, and the world are our enemies.

Deliverance is a process. The basis of our scriptural authority to break generational curses that may be upon us is found in Galatians 3:13:

Christ redeemed us from the curse of the law by becoming a curse for us, for it is written: "Cursed is everyone who is hung on a tree." He redeemed us in order that the blessing given to Abraham might come to the Gentiles through Christ Jesus, (Galatians 3:13).

Once we declare the curse to be broken, we can expel the demons who have tried to enforce the curse. Later in this booklet, we will show you how to free yourself and your children from the effects of idolatry-related curses that may be operating in your family line.

WHAT IS IDOLATRY?

Perhaps you once adored, venerated, or were devoted to the Queen of Heaven. Perhaps you are shocked to hear that God considers it idolatry, especially when you feel that you performed your devotions out of a love for God and Jesus Christ. Many ancient Israelites may also have felt that God approved of their devotions to the Queen of Heaven.

Many people are deeply hurt, offended, or feel misunderstood if someone suggests that their Marian devotion may be idolatrous. Several sincere believers have been taught from childhood that God is pleased when they "honor His Mother," and they sincerely believe that they perform these devotions in accordance with God's will. They may maintain that they do not actually worship the Queen of Heaven the way they worship God. Rather, they maintain that they are simply venerating, adoring, honoring, and performing devotions to her. Many are well-intentioned believers with a sincere love for Christ. Still, Jesus Himself said,

"It is written: 'Worship the Lord your God and serve him only'" (Luke 4:8).

Webster's Dictionary defines "worship" in this manner:

Worship n. Reverence for a sacred object or personage; high esteem or devotion for a person. v. to revere; attend a religious service. A synonym for the word worship is honor, revere, adore, idolize, reverence.[4]

More importantly, God defines idolatry clearly in Scripture. We must not bend the knee or trust in any created being other than God Himself.

But ye shall destroy their altars, break their images, and cut down their groves: For thou shalt worship no other god: for the LORD, whose name *is* Jealous, *is* a jealous God (Exodus 34:13-14 KJV).

Some church teachers say that there are several Latin words that denote different levels of worship, and that the highest type is reserved for the Trinity alone. Regardless of word games, many cross the line into idolatry when they trust Mary to do for them what only God Himself can do.

For only God is omniscient (all-knowing), omnipotent (all-powerful), and omnipresent (everywhere at all times). He will not share His Glory with another.

Jesus is the only mediator that God has provided, and He is all we need.

THE FORCE BEHIND THE IDOL

As well as being a high-level demonic world ruler, the Queen of Heaven system also represents a whole structure of evil, a vast demonic hierarchy of malevolent spirits intent on corrupting biblical faith and practice.

Although someone can be deceived and still be one of God's elect assured of Heaven, many need to realize that even idolatry committed in ignorance can bring terrible consequences in this life, or to one's children.

The Scriptures are clear that even if someone does not mean to open their heart to demonic influence, they still can unwittingly:

"If a person sins, and commits any of these things which are forbidden to be done by the commandments of the LORD, though he does not know it, yet he is guilty and shall bear his iniquity" (Leviticus 5:17 NKJV).

Preachers of righteousness will always lead people in the ways of God, His Word, and His Spirit through Jesus Christ. We must turn from all sin, and, through repentance and faith, return to the Lord and trust in His sacrifice for us at Calvary alone. God is raising up teachers who will proclaim the truth to all the world and to all who will listen.

"'And they shall teach My people the difference between the holy and the unholy, and cause them to discern between the unclean and the clean'" (Ezekial 44:23 NKJV).

GODDESS OF DECEPTION

In the Christian world, every time the "Queen" appears in a major historic apparition, she gives extra non-scriptural theology that is soon introduced in the Church. In the secular world, she can just as easily lie and change her "name" and appear, for example, to Mohammed, thus sparking Islam. Or she can appear to Joseph Smith and inaugurate Mormonism. The devil is a deceiver.

How tragic to be unable to see through her deceptions. My prayer is that this booklet will open your eyes to this ancient deception and will result in your faith being centered on Christ alone.

The apostle Paul wrote to the church in Greece, a main center of goddess worship, saying,

I am jealous for you with a godly jealousy. I promised you to one husband, to Christ [not to his "mother!"], **so that I might present you as a pure virgin** [undefiled by idolatry...faithful to Him alone] **to him. But I am afraid that just as Eve was deceived by the serpent's cunning, your minds may somehow be led astray from your sincere and pure devotion to Christ.** [We do not need "devotion" to anyone other than Christ.] **For if someone comes to you and preaches a Jesus other than the Jesus we preached, or if you**

receive a different spirit from the one you received, or a different gospel from the one you accepted, you put up with it easily enough (2 Corinthians 11:2-4; emphasis mine).

The apparition's teachings bring about root errors:

1. that faith in Christ alone is not enough to be saved;
2. that one must also embrace her doctrine and obey her decrees.

When this apparition appears to deceive believers, the apparition takes a little Christian theology and mixes it with idolatry and error. This blending of truth and error is called "syncretism," making it easier to be deceived, especially:

1. if this demon has already found a home in your family line,
2. if you have not studied the Scriptures in depth,
3. if you have believed blindly what certain men have proclaimed.

The Bible exhorts us to study God's Word to show ourselves approved and to rightly handle the Word of truth.

Evidently some people are throwing you into confusion and are trying to pervert the gospel of Christ. But even if we or an angel from heaven should preach a gospel other than the one we preached to you, let him be eternally condemned! As we have already said, so now I say again: If anybody is preaching to you a gospel other than what you accepted, let him be eternally condemned! (Galatians 1:7-9).

If one reads the Scripture, and understands the simplicity of the gospel, it becomes easy to see the addition of the unnecessary teachings of the Mother goddess spirit.

THE GOSPEL OF JESUS CHRIST

> …if you confess with your mouth, "Jesus is Lord," and believe in your heart that God raised him from the dead, you will be saved. For it is with your heart that you believe and are justified, and it is with your mouth that you confess and are saved. As the Scripture says, "Anyone who trusts in him will never be put to shame." For there is no difference between Jew and Gentile—the same Lord is Lord of all and richly blesses all who call on him, for, "Everyone who calls on the name of the Lord will be saved" (Romans 10:9-13).

> The Gospel of John says it most clearly:
> **For God so loved the world that he gave his one and only Son, that whoever believes in him shall not perish but have eternal life. For God did not send his Son into the world to condemn the world, but to save the world through him. Whoever believes in him is not condemned, but whoever does not believe stands condemned already because he has not believed in the name of God's one and only Son (John 3:16).**

Notice the Scripture does not say that we are to believe in the name of God's one and only *Mother* to be saved!

No believer needs to be afraid that if they don't obey "Mary" they will be punished, or miss out on some great reward. Christ has already purchased your salvation, sanctification, and acceptance before the Father. You do not need mediators, scapulars, devotions to Mary, or any religious tool to be in right standing with the Father.

> **For it is by grace you have been saved, through faith—and this not from yourselves, it is the gift of God—not by works, so that no one can boast (Ephesians 2:8-9).**

> **For there is one God and one mediator between God and men, the man Christ Jesus, who gave himself as a ransom for all men (1 Timothy 2:5-6).**

NOTES

[1] George Otis Jr., public speech at converence, USA.

[2] Rev. L.M. Dooley, S.V.D., *That Motherly Mother of Guadelupe* (Massachusetts: The Daughters of St. Paul, 1979) pp. 20-21.

[3] Ibid, p. 37.

[4] "Worship", Webster's New World Dictionary, (Simon and Schuster, Inc., 1990) p. 683.

Chapter Three

THE APPARITIONS OF "MARY"

> They are spirits of demons performing miraculous signs... (Revelation 16:14).

Although Asherah appeared throughout the ancient world, she changed her name to "Mary" and began to deceive uninformed Christians and others around 250 A.D.

THE FALSE MARY APPEARS

- A.D. 250 - First recorded apparition - to Gregory the "wonderworker"
- A.D. 300 - Le Puy, France
- A.D. 700 - Evesham, England
- A.D. 1150 - St. Elizabeth of Schonau. (She had a vision of "Mary" being assumed bodily into heaven, and this doctrine was released into the Church's theology.)
- A.D. 1251 - Simon Stock receives the scapular by "Our

> Lady of Mt. Carmel" (the same principality that opposed Elijah with her "husband" Ba'al on the same mountain)

A.D. 1347 - St. Catherine of Sienna
A.D. 1490 - Genoa, Italy
A.D. 1531 - Guadelupe, Mexico
A.D. 1858 - Lourdes, France
A.D. 1917 - Fatima, Portugal
A.D. 1961 - Garabandal, Spain (where she truly exposed herself as an abusive mother)
A.D. 1981 - Medugorge, Yugoslavia, 21st century—where next?

OUR LADY OF GUADELUPE, MEXICO, 1531

As the Queen of Heaven saw her kingdom being threatened in Europe by the Protestant Reformation, she appeared in Mexico to reassert her power in the New World. Her appearance here was to launch her into a truly world-wide ministry of deception.

On the feast day of the Immaculate Conception, an Aztec Indian, Juan Diego, whose ancestors had made sacrifices to this same Aztec goddess, was on his way to celebrate her feast day in Guadelupe, Mexico, on December 9, 1531.

There was a hill on his way to the local church that had been the site of sacrifices and worship to the Mother goddess. The hill was called Tepeyac, and on it had stood a temple the Aztecs had erected to the Queen of Heaven when she had appeared to them in a previous guise.

It was a temple to the Virgin Mother goddess Tonantzin, who was known as the "Little Mother" to the Aztecs there. She was a favorite goddess, since she

The Apparitions of Mary

appeared as a young, beautiful woman and promised mercy if she was obeyed.

Juan Diego saw the apparition on her hill. Of course, one of her first requests was that another temple be erected in her honor on this same hill of her previous temple.

She lied to him and said,

"I am the Ever-Virgin Mary, Mother of the true God... it is my wish that a temple be built here to me on this site. Here, as the loving Mother of you and your fellow men, I will show forth my loving kindness and compassion for your people and for those who love me and seek me, and call upon me in their labors and afflictions. Here I will comfort and assuage.

Do not let anything worry you... .Am I not here, I who am your Mother? Are you not under my shadow and protection? Am I not your life and health? Are you not in my embrace and in my prayers? What else do you need?[1]

Now, if Juan Diego had known the Scriptures, he would have recognized the blasphemy and error of this message. He would have walked away from the spirit who was seeking his devotion and worship. He would have seen through her attempt to usurp God's place.

But Juan did not know the Scriptures. So, he embraced the spirit and she gained entrance again into the Church once more through him. He became her mouthpiece. He was subject to her deception because his people had worshiped the "Little Mother" for centuries and had made a pact with her, perpetuated by ceremony and consecration. This demon felt she had a legal right to appear to him and deceive him in this manner.

The deception, of course, is evident to the biblically literate. This ancient Asherah wanted a throne. She wanted a temple. She wanted images and idols made of her. She wanted people to open their hearts to her and allow her access. She desired that prayers meant for God alone be addressed to her. And she tells us today that we need nothing else but devotion to her. She not-so-subtly suggests that she is equal, or even more important, than God Himself!

She then performed a great sign for Juan Diego. The "Queen" produced fragrant roses out of season and arranged them in the folds of his mantle. Later, in the presence of leaders of the Church, as the roses fell to the floor, they left an image of the Lady, a supernatural portrait of the woman exactly as Juan had seen her. This image, made on a cloak of cactus cloth (which has a normal life span of twenty years before it decays), is still vibrant with the supernatural image 450 years later!

Many Christians say that Satan cannot do miracles. But this is not true:

He [Satan and his demons] **performs great signs.... And he deceives those who dwell on the earth by those signs which he was granted to do... (Revelation 13:13-14 NKJV).**

Remember the magicians in Pharaoh's court? They were also able to counterfeit many miracles through demonic power.

They are spirits of demons performing miraculous signs... (Revelation 16:14).

The Apparitions of Mary

The Aztec Indians, who had worshiped the Virgin Mother in their ancestry, were eager to obey this apparition's commands. Millions of Mexicans were converted to devotion to her. But how many were actually converted to faith in Christ?

Church statistics claim that almost eight million Mexicans came to give her their hearts within seven years. Their hearts were already inclined favorably towards the Mother goddess.

But it was not Miriam, the real Mother of Jesus. It was Asherah, the ancient Mother goddess and deceiver of men. Even today, multitudes from all over the world, even Christian people, come to Guadelupe to ask favors of this spirit.

APPARITION OF FATIMA, PORTUGAL, 1917

> …he even makes fire come down from heaven on the earth in the sight of men. And he deceives those who dwell on the earth by those signs which he was granted to do… (Revelation 13:13-14 NKJV).

In 1917, Asherah appeared again and did mighty miracles in the sight of many people. Here in Fatima, Portugal, the "Queen of Heaven" appeared once more.

Three children, aged seven, nine, and ten, were in a pasture when a powerful spirit appeared to them. The spirit said he was "Michael, the Archangel." He brought an unscriptural message to them, saying that, through their suffering, they could pay God back for the sins that others had committed.

Asherah appeared to the children and declared herself to be an important personage, even the Mother of God.

Her message progressed with each visit and became more self-serving. Eventually, she declared that only she could save the world and that reparation was now needed for sins against her!

Fatima included the supernatural appearance of fire from heaven, as well as visual miracles of the sun actually "dancing" across the sky. This miracle was witnessed by many people. She also performed occult healings. Finally, a spring of water shot up, amazing many people.

The record of the apparitions of the "False Mary" (Asherah) throughout the Church age are too numerous to mention. Recently, this spirit has also appeared in Medugorge, in the former Yugoslavia, and now even in America.

Asherah gained a stronger throne in the Lord's Church when the Pope in 1964 proclaimed her the "Mother of the Church," and placed it under her care. The United States has been formally dedicated to her through vow and ceremony. The Pope himself has formally consecrated the entire world to her in a public ceremony. Although he may have had the best of intentions, what are the consequences of such an action? Jesus said,

"I tell you the truth, whatever you bind on earth will be bound in heaven, and whatever you loose on earth will be loosed in heaven" (Matthew 18:18).

Soon, we will come to the final showdown between the spirit of the Anti-Christ and the Spirit of the Lord. We are living in exciting times! We can expect to see more of the activity of the Queen of Heaven before the end comes. Ultimately, Scripture tells us that she will indeed be punished by the Lord Himself. Interestingly, the apparition has been talking a lot about a great punishment coming. This is true—only the punishment that is coming is her own. That is why all those who are still in her must leave, before His judgment falls on her systems.

> **What agreement is there between the temple of God and idols? For we are the temple of the living God. As God has said: "I will live with them and walk among them, and I will be their God, and they will be my people."**
>
> **"Therefore come out from them and be separate, says the Lord. Touch no unclean thing, and I will receive you." "I will be a Father to you, and you will be my sons and daughters, says the Lord Almighty" (2 Corinthians 6:16-18).**

NOTES

[1] Rev. L.M. Dooley, S.V.D., *That Motherly Mother of Guadelupe* (Massachusetts: The Daughters of St. Paul, 1979) pp. 20-21.

Chapter Four

GOSPEL ACCORDING TO ASHTORETH

> Your word is a lamp to my feet and a
> light for my path (Psalm 119:105).

The Holy Bible is one of the surest guides we have in this life. It is the standard by which we measure all revelations, opinions, or experiences. The Scriptures say in 2 Timothy 3:15-17,

> **…from infancy you have known the holy Scriptures, which are able to make you wise for salvation through faith in Christ Jesus. All Scripture is God-breathed and is useful for teaching, rebuking, correcting and training in righteousness, so that the man of God may be thoroughly equipped for every good work.**

Every person should read and study God's Holy Word, for it can protect us from all error of doctrine or practice. And as we seek Him and desire His correction and guidance in our lives, His Spirit will lead us.

Be diligent to present yourself approved to God, a worker who does not need to be ashamed, rightly dividing the word of truth (2 Timothy 2:15 NKJV).

One main reason that the spirit of Asherah can deceive is because many Christians do not study or really know the doctrines taught in the Bible. Instead, they become prey to the "Doctrines of Asherah." We also do not understand history as we ought.

Dear friends, do not believe every spirit, but test the spirits to see whether they are from God, because many false prophets have gone out into the world (1 John 4:1).

Here are some of "Mary's" words that believers must judge to be lies and deception. They point to her attempt to make herself equal to God:

WORDS OF MARY

"One day through the Rosary and Scapular, I will save the world" - to St. Dominic

I am begging you to give yourself to me so that I can offer you as a gift to god, fresh and without sin....
- Lady of Medugorge, August 1, 1985

I call upon you to open yourselves completely to me....
- Lady of Medugorge, November 25, 1994

Come closer to my immaculate heart and you will discover god.... - Lady of Medugorge, November 25, 1994

My presence here is to lead you on a new path.... -Lady of Medugorge, June 25, 1992

The rosary alone can do miracles in the world and in your lives.... - Lady of Medugorge, January 25, 1991

I invite you to dedicate your life to me...surrender everything completely to me.... - Lady of Medugorge, November, 27, 1986

It is important that you renounce and break any consecrations made to this spirit. Curses may be released down through the generations when idolatry of any type is committed. Without repentance, this demon thinks it has a legal right to harass, even though you may have become a Christian.

> **"Repent! Turn away from all your offenses; then sin will not be your downfall. Rid yourselves of all the offenses you have committed, and get a new heart and a new spirit" (Ezekial 18:30-31).**

Repentance is a foundation of our walk with the Lord. We need to have a repentant heart of love and humility.

The Bible tells us that all have sinned and fall short of God's glory. Even Jesus' earthly mother needed a savior. Even if you feel you are a good person, you must realize that your goodness is still not enough to atone for your

Gospel According to Ashtoreth

sinful nature deep inside of you. Only the blood of Christ can atone for your sinful nature, and you must put your faith in His sacrifice on the cross alone to be saved.

Maybe you realize how much of a sinner you are. Perhaps you have tried to be better, or have made sacrifices to atone for your sin. Perhaps you have tried to obey Mary's commands to improve yourself.

The Queen of Heaven cannot help you, and you don't need her. She is not God. The Scriptures say,

> **Therefore, since we have a great high priest who has gone through the heavens, Jesus the Son of God, let us hold firmly to the faith we profess. For we do not have a high priest who is unable to sympathize with our weaknesses, but we have one who has been tempted in every way, just as we are—yet was without sin. Let us then approach the throne of grace with confidence, so that we may receive mercy and find grace to help us in our time of need (Hebrews 4:14).**

True salvation is only found in Him. Faith in Jesus is all you need. God is calling you to put your trust in Him, and to call out to Him, inviting His Holy Spirit to come into you. This is done by accepting Jesus as your Lord, and then confessing this fact aloud.

The Bible says,

> **That if you confess with your mouth, "Jesus is Lord," and believe in your heart that God raised him from the dead, you will be saved (Romans 10:9).**

Won't you turn to Jesus anew right now, even as you are reading these words? Please pray this prayer, and mean it from your heart, especially if you have never confessed this truth aloud before to God. Confess to Him now that you are a sinner separated from His power, love, and holiness.

Dear God, I confess that I am a sinner. I ask You to forgive me. I accept Your only Son Jesus as my Savior and master. I believe that He died for my sins. Lord Jesus, save me! Have mercy on me! Come into my heart right now, and make me new!

Chapter Five

STEPS TO FREEDOM FROM GENERATIONAL CURSES OF MARIANISM

1. Reject and renounce all Marian doctrines, traditions, and influences in your life.
2. Ask God in prayer to forgive you for offending Him and repent of the sin of idolatry.
3. Re-affirm your faith in Christ alone and your simple devotion to Him. Trust that Jesus is the only mediator that the Father has provided for you and that He is all you need.
4. Study God's Word, the Bible, and learn about what really pleases God.
5. Destroy or throw away all rosary beads, scapulars, statues of Mary, miraculous medals, pictures of the Queen …anything that may link you with this principality, even if it is a treasured family heirloom.
6. Break the curse of idolatry through prayer.
7. Pray to accept Christ as your Lord and Savior.

8. Bind every demon spirit that may have entered your life through Marian connections or involvement of any type. Cast these demons out, in Jesus name.
9. Share these "Steps of Freedom" with others.

We have provided some other basic tools in this booklet for you. First, is a prayer of renunciation, and then lastly, there is a list of demons most commonly found in families with Marianism in it. The list is not meant to be exhaustive; it is merely a starting point for deliverance prayer.

To break possible Marian curses, pray the following:

Prayer of Renunciation and Release

(Pray this prayer alone and aloud, or with another present)

Heavenly Father, I come before You now and ask to be released from all righteous curses involved with generational iniquity in my family line, specifically coming from idolatry or witchcraft of any type, including Marianism or Freemasonry. In Your Word, You declare,

I am the LORD thy God, which have brought thee out of the land of Egypt, out of the house of bondage. Thou shalt have no other gods before me. Thou shalt not make unto thee any graven image, or any likeness of any thing that is in heaven above, or that is in the earth beneath, or that is in the water under the earth: Thou shalt not bow down thyself to them, nor serve them: for I the LORD thy God am a jealous God, visiting the iniquity of the fathers upon the children unto the

third and fourth generation of them that hate [me] **(Exodus 20:2-5 KJV).**

I renounce and repent of any idolatry in my family line, for my parents, grandparents, and great-grandparents, and I renounce and repent of any sin of idolatry or blasphemy that they may have knowingly or unknowingly committed.

RENUNCIATION OF THE QUEEN OF HEAVEN

Father, concerning Mary, the mother of Jesus, I call her blessed as Scripture declares, for the wondrous part she played in your plan of salvation. But I renounce the deification of her, the doctrine that she was born without original sin, and the doctrine that she was ascended into heaven and crowned the Queen of Heaven. I renounce any false teachings which opened up my ancestors, or myself, into committing idolatry.

I also renounce the spirit behind the false doctrine, and the spirit behind the Apparitions of "the Queen" throughout history, which has sought to deceive God's children.

Father, I repent because of my ancestors' involvement with the World Ruler known as the "Queen of Heaven," "Our Lady," or the "Mother of God." I ask you to forgive me, and to cleanse my family line (me and my children) from the effects of the idolatry-related curses of Deuteronomy 28:15-68, especially, poverty, female problems, divorce, breakdown of family relationships, emotional distress, depression, anxiety or panic, defeat, failure, mental torment or confusion, ongoing traumas, accidents, emotional hardness, "control" spirit or religious spirit, premature death, spiritual hindrances, doubt, skepticism, unbelief, mockery, intellectualism, pride or arrogance, or any of the curses listed in Scripture that come down the generation when there has been idolatry. I declare aloud the truth of Galatians 3:13:

> **Christ redeemed us from the curse of the law by becoming a curse for us, for it is written: "Cursed is everyone who is hung on a tree." He redeemed us in order that the blessing given to Abraham might come to the Gentiles through Christ Jesus, so that by faith we might receive the promise of the Spirit.**

I renounce the following doctrines of demons that may have led me or my ancestors into idolatry:

I renounce the doctrine which says,

1. **"Mary's role as co-redemptrix did not cease with the glorification of her Son."**
   John Paul II, Allocution at the Sanctuary of Our Lady of Guayaquil, given on Jan 31, 1985, reported in Osservatore Romano Supplement of February 2, 1985.

I affirm that the Word of God states,

> **Salvation is found in no one else [but Jesus], for there is no other name under heaven given to men by which we must be saved" (Acts 4:12).**

I renounce the doctrine which says,

2. **"... it is right to say, that nothing is imparted to us except through Mary, since God so wills, so that just as no one can come to the Father except through the**

Son, so in general, no one can come to Christ except through His Mother."

Leo XIII, Encyclical, Octobri mense adventante, September 22, 1891, ASS 24, 1891.

I, again, affirm that the Word of God states,

Salvation is found in no one else [but Jesus], for there is no other name under heaven given to men by which we must be saved (Acts 4:12).

I renounce the doctrine which says,

3. "The Immaculate Virgin, preserved free from all stain of original sin, when the course of her earthly life was finished, was taken up body and soul into heavenly glory, and exalted by the Lord as Queen over all things"

Official Catechism of the Catholic Church

The Word of God declares that,

…all have sinned and fall short of the glory of God… (Romans 3:23).

I renounce the doctrine which says,

4. **The Mother of God, the Virgin Mary, is the treasurer (sequestra) of our peace with God, and the mediatrix (administra) of graces…."**

Leo XIII, Encyclical, Supremi Apostolatus officio. September 1, 1883. ASS 16, 1883. 1113.

I declare that God created all things, and has no mother over Him, nor a Queen that rules with Him, and that,

…there is one God and one mediator between God and men, the man Christ Jesus (1 Timothy 2:5).

I renounce the doctrine which says,

5. **"…her kingdom is as vast as that of her Son and God, since nothing is excluded from her dominion."**
   18) Pius XII, Radiomessage to Fatima, Bendito seja, May 13, 1946, AAS 38, 19465, 266:

I renounce the doctrine which says,

6. **"The Church's devotion to the Blessed Virgin is an intrinsic element of Christian worship."**
   Paul VI also, in his Apostolic Exhortation, Marialis cultus, of Feb. 2, 1974, AAS 66 # 56 .

The Scripture says,

For you are great and do marvelous deeds; you alone are God (Psalm 86:10).

I hereby renounce all Marian doctrine; I break all consecrations over me and my children to the Queen of Heaven.

I promise to destroy or throw away all magical amulets such as the scapular, miraculous medal, Mary statues, and rosary beads, as well as pictures of her.

Steps to Freedom from Generational Curses of Marianism

Take a moment. Break all Marian consecrations off, and bind every spirit associated with those curses, and dismiss them, in Jesus name. The most common demons associated with Marianism are found in the next section.

Appendix

DELIVERANCE PRAYER GUIDE

> And these signs will accompany those who believe: In my name they will drive out demons… they will speak in new tongue… they will place their hands on sick people, and they will get well (Mark 16:17-18).

This is a guide to some of the most common demons that may be afflicting the life of a person getting free from the Queen of Heaven. Although all of us may have experienced oppression from these demons, those with Marian roots in their family may experience these things more strongly.

Scripture teaches that as people we have three parts. This is known as the "Tripartite" view of human nature. We have a spirit, a soul, and a body. That is why Paul prayed that we would be kept blameless in body, soul, and spirit. Let's look at each briefly and see how a demon could affect us.

When someone becomes a Christian and experiences an authentic conversion and becomes born-again, their spirit become one with the Lord. Praise God! After that, demons in the soul realm may not be ultimately successful in bringing us to hell, but they sure can make our life on earth a "living hell"!

All people also have a soul. The soul is comprised of the mind (thought-life), the will, and the emotions. And of course, we all have a physical body.

The soul, the mind, the emotions, and the will, as well as the physical body, is the battle ground. The devil can tempt, harass, afflict, oppress, torment, persecute, and try to destroy. The soul and body realm is what is being fought over when a believer receives deliverance prayer. Notice, a born-again believer cannot be demon-possessed, as their spirit is one with the Lord. But they *can* have certain areas of their soul demonized, or demon-influenced. This is the source of temptation. The demonic takes advantage of the fallen flesh to induce us to dishonor God's temple and violate His precepts.

Here is a list of the demons that can affect the mind, emotions, will, or body of a person—even a believer. This is *NOT* a comprehensive list, but it is merely a place to begin:

Asherah, Isis, Queen of Heaven, Sorrowful Mother, Eye of Horus, Python, Leviathan, Sorrow, Despair, Despondency, Hopelessness, Depression, Worry, Anxiety, Fears, Nervousness, Confusion, Doubt, Pride, Affectation, Mimicry, False Burden, Over-Responsibility, Legalism, Death, Sickness, Inherited demons, Cursing, Sexual Impurity, Harlotry, Cults, Occult, Magic, Witchcraft, Spiritism, Rejection, Perfection, Error, Mind-Control, Spiritual Dullness, Physical Pain, Poverty, Rage, Revenge, Unforgiveness, Bitterness, Rebellion.

Bind each spirit named above, and cast them out of your thoughts, emotions, or body, in Jesus name and out loud, and with confidence and faith. The demons will recognize the Lord's authority within you and will obey.

Steps to Effective Deliverance:

1. Confess and renounce sins
2. Extend forgiveness to all others
3. Break curses
4. Break soul ties. (Soul ties are soulish bonds to other people. They may be edifying, or they may not be. Ask God to show you what relationships affect you negatively, and then ask Him to sever it. You can still have a relationship with someone that you once had an ungodly soul tie with. You will know the freedom when the soul tie is broken. Ask Him to strengthen the godly soul ties in your life. Sin always strengthens ungodly soul ties and weakens godly soul ties.)
5. Expel demons, one by one, by name.

(Some of the following material is abridged from: Eckhardt, John. *Identifying and Breaking Curses.* Crusaders Ministries, 1999.)

Some Reasons that Deliverance Is Delayed

1. Unbroken curses
2. Unrepentant sin
3. Pride
4. Passive; will not cooperate in the deliverance session
5. Ungodly soul ties
6. Still involved in occult activity.
7. Embarrassment

8. Unbelief
9. Rebellious, and not under authority
10. Lack of desire
11. Unforgiveness

(Some of the following material abridged from *"Identifying and Breaking Curses'* Eckhardt, John, Crusaders Ministries, 1999)

SIGNS OF EFFECTIVE DELIVERANCE OCCURRING

It is always best if someone on the deliverance team is fasting. Using all the gifts of the Spirit will facilitate a good deliverance result.

When evil spirits actually leave the emotions, thoughts, will, or body of someone, you can normally expect some type of manifestation, usually through the mouth, nose, or eyes. It comes from the breath, which means "pneuma," or spirit. Just as Jesus breathed on them to impart the Holy Spirit, often demons can depart with an exhalation of breath, since they are spirits, which means "breath." Breath in the Holy Spirit and breath out the demons!

Here are the most common signs that demons are leaving:

1. Coughing
2. Screaming, wailing, shrieking
3. Spitting, vomiting, or drooling
4. Crying, tears
5. Sighing, yawning, exhaling
6. Belching

Manifestations that may signal a demon's presence, but do not mean the demon is actually leaving:

1. Violent contortions
2. Cursing
3. Trembling or shaking
4. Physical pain, headache, backache, etc.
5. Eyes rolling up in head
6. Incoherence, unable to talk
7. Going into a trance

Again, the demons should come out from the mouth or nose, or eyes.

It is good to lay hands on a person receiving deliverance, as well as to anoint them with oil afterwards, as the Spirit leads, as a symbol of them rededicating their temple to the Lord.

HOW TO KEEP WALKING IN FREEDOM

1. Deliverance is an ongoing process. Be patient—we may battle these spirits for a long time, although they will weaken and have less influence. Some leave immediately and forever, others try to come back in later through sin.
2. Read God's Word regularly.
3. Join a Spirit-filled church and meet with others for worship, teaching, and ministering to others.
4. Ask the Lord to baptize you afresh with the Holy Spirit.
5. Know which demon spirits afflict, tempt, or harass you. Become determined to fight them and to not allow them to re-enter.
6. Realize that the thought-life is the battleground. Ask the Lord to crucify your carnal mind, since we are indeed crucified with Christ. Ask Him that His mind would arise within you.

7. You can tell they are trying to return when old thought patterns return. Speak out loud to them, bind them, and cast them away.

ABOUT THE AUTHOR

Vinny Gallagher is the founder and senior pastor of Mercy Christian Fellowship and School of the Spirit, in Phoenixville, Pennsylvania.

He is completing his Doctoral degree in Ministry and holds a Master's degree from Denver Seminary and a Bachelor's degree from Eastern College.

He has taught at Seminary of the East, an Evangelical Theology school, as well as at Eastern College in their Graduate Counseling program and their undergraduate Psychology and Youth Ministry departments.

He has authored three books and has been interviewed on dozens of Christian radio stations across the country.

Before planting Mercy Christian Fellowship, he served the Church as a professional counselor at Minirth-Meir Life Counseling Services. Prior to that, he served on the pastoral staff of several churches.

He is a member of the International Coalition of Apostles led by Dr. C. Peter Wagner.

Order Form

To order *Exposing the Queen of Heaven,* please use the order form below (please print):

Name: _____

Address: _____

City: _____ State/Prov: _____

Zip/Postal Code: _____ Telephone: _____

* COPIES ARE $8.00 US OR $12.00 CDN EACH.
** 3 OR MORE COPIES ARE $6.00 US OR $9.00 CDN EACH.

____ copies @ $ ____ US / Cdn = $_____

A videotape presentation on *Exposing the Queen of Heaven* is available. It is 30 minutes long, professionally done with illustrations, and is great for the education of church groups or individuals.

____ videos @ $10.00 US / $15.00 Cdn = $_____

Shipping: ($3.00 first book/video – $1.00 each add. bk./vid.) $_____

Total amount enclosed: $_____

Payable by Check or Postal Money Order

(Please make checks payable to Vinny Gallagher.
Allow time for checks to clear.)

Send to: Vinny Gallagher
             Box 123
             Honey Brook, Pennsylvania
             19344-0123
             (610) 415-0115
             E-mail: Jesuslovesu4ever@juno.com
             Web site: www.mercyfellowship.org